THE LITTLE BOOK OF
MONEY

THE LITTLE BOOK OF
MONEY

*A Guide to Managing Your
Finances, Building Your Wealth,
and Investing in Yourself*

LEAH N. MILES

DRIVEN

Copyright © 2023 by Penguin Random House LLC

All rights reserved.

Published in the United States by Driven, an imprint of Zeitgeist™, a division of Penguin Random House LLC, New York.

penguinrandomhouse.com

ISBN: 9780593673867

Produced by Girl Friday Productions

Book design by Rachel Marek
Illustrations by Sam Michaels

Printed in the United States of America

1st Printing

Image credits (all credits belong to Shutterstock users, except where noted): Cover (main), Sigridstock; Cover (money jar), Chones; ii, moon phase photo; viii, Aumpattarawut; x, rafastockbr; 2, Troggt; 10, Alexey Stiop; 14, jason cox; 18, 279photo Studio; 24, NORTHFOLK / Unsplash; 27, littlesam; 29, Nataliya Vaitkevich / Pexels; 34, hedgehog94; 37, brizmaker; 40, fizkes; 46, ANNVIPS; 49, V_L; 50, Marie C Fields; 51, Proxima Studio; 52, fizkes; 54, Have a nice day Photo; 58, lupmotion; 66, Elena Elisseeva; 70, MosayMay; 72, Leka Sergeeva; 74, twggy; 76, nampix; 78, Christina Vartanova; 81, Nattapat.J; 84, Ursula Page

CONTENTS

"A wise person should have money in their head, but not in their heart."

—JONATHAN SWIFT

INTRODUCTION

W hat are your financial dreams and goals for the future? Do you want to travel the world? Buy your family the perfect house? Take care of your parents in their old age? Feel free of debt and secure no matter what life throws your way?

Money has value because it reflects what you value. All too often we can get swept up in the hamster wheel of *work, pay bills, sleep, repeat*. We feel like we live to work rather than work to live. But getting control of your money and making it work for you can give you freedom and agency in what can otherwise seem like an impersonal and joyless system.

Your financial well-being is just as important as your physical and mental well-being. It's time to start caring for it, because it's part of you, too.

This little book is a great place to start. It begins with a quick run-through of the basics of banking, and then it turns to budgeting—a weighted term that really means putting you in confident control of your financial life. The final section offers ideas to spark your own plans for growing your wealth. Recurring sidebars offer you opportunities to both challenge and treat yourself. Challenges allow you to stretch and reach your financial goals in fun and interesting ways. Treats give you simple ideas for recharging, mentally, physically, and

socially–without spending a dime. After all, the best things in life are free, right? Remember: building wealth is a worthy endeavor, but you need to take care of yourself first.

This little book is just that–a small glimpse of what is a wide world of finances and potential. It's no substitute for expert financial advice. Markets, strategies, investment vehicles, jobs, taxes, regulations, and more are ever changing and much, much bigger than this little book can cover. However, we hope it gives you a spark of inspiration–and the confidence in yourself–to seek expert advice, do your own research into your area's specific regulations and opportunities, and take control of your financial health.

MONEY IN YOUR POCKET

Mastering Everyday Finances

Somewhere along the line, your piggy bank could no longer hold all the money you earned (good job, you!), and your first bank account became your entry into the world of financial institutions. In this section, we'll talk about banking basics as a foundation for growing wealth and achieving financial goals.

All About That Bank

Banks manage money and how it moves between people, places, and businesses. They offer a range of financial services, from a straightforward checking account to a high-yield savings account to a car loan. Banks can have brick-and-mortar locations, or they can be online institutions. Either way, to protect your money and grow your wealth, you'll need a bank.

Here, we'll explore some banking basics, like traditional accounts and interest rates.

Why Put Your Money in a Bank?

- **It's safer than a safe.** Banks protect your money with specially designed systems against theft. No need to worry about anyone finding your hiding spot or cracking open your piggy bank.
- **It's insured.** Most deposits to banks are insured. You automatically get FDIC or NCUA insurance when you open an account at a bank or credit union. This means that if your bank or credit union folds, you'll get your money back.
- **It's protected from damage and natural disasters.** Banks can better protect money in a fire, flood, or other natural disaster, plus their insurance will cover any problems (whereas homeowners' insurance might not).

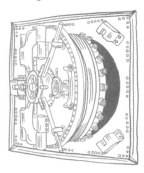

CHECKING ACCOUNTS

One of the most common accounts opened at a bank is a checking account. It's an account that you can put a sum of money into and then draw from for basic everyday transactions. You can put money into a checking account via ATM deposit, mobile deposit, electronic or wire transfers, direct deposit, or in-person deposit with a bank teller. You can take money out of a checking account at an ATM or with a debit card, a check, or an electronic or wire transfer.

A standard checking account will do for most daily transactions, but banks offer a variety of checking options. Here are a few of the variations. Be sure to talk to your bank about what's right for you.

- **Interest checking** offers the opportunity to earn interest on the balance in the account.
- **Student checking** welcomes college-age newcomers to the banking world with fewer fees and some reward perks.
- **Senior checking** offers a variety of personalization options and perks for folks 65 years and older.
- **Second chance checking** allows folks with less-than-stellar banking history to hold accounts (usually with higher fees) and potentially earn their way back to a standard account.

Interested in Interest Rates?

Interest is a percentage charged for borrowed money. So, when someone is talking about an interest rate, it depends, interestingly, on what type of transaction they're referring to and who the borrower is. When you open an interest checking or savings account, the interest rate is a percentage of your initial deposit *the bank will give to you* on top of your investment in return for keeping your money there for a given time. That period is usually a year, so banks often use the abbreviation APY, for annual percentage yield. For example, if you deposit $1,000 in a savings account with a 0.07% interest rate per year, your balance at the end of the year will be $1,000.70. Some savings accounts also offer compound interest, which means you earn interest on your interest if you don't withdraw your money before whatever the compounding period is. See *Interest and APR* on page 14 to see what interest rates mean for credit card and loan transactions.

Treat Yourself—for Free: Host a get-together. You don't need to spend a fortune to have a potluck, hold a game night, do a movie marathon, have a friendly baking competition, create your own home spa for a girls' night, or invite people over for other inventive reasons. Just call up a few friends, ask each one to bring something (or don't!), and have fun.

SAVINGS ACCOUNTS

Unlike a checking account, which is designed to hold money that will be spent in the short term, a savings account is meant to store money over a longer period and even grow your initial investment. Where a checking account offers little to no interest, a savings account will give you a higher interest rate, but you may have limits on how much or how often you can withdraw money from the account.

HIGH-YIELD SAVINGS ACCOUNTS

Much like a traditional savings account, a high-yield savings account stores money over a longer term and offers a chance to grow your investment through interest rates. However, the big difference is the interest rate, or APY. Though a traditional savings account might have an APY of 0.07%, high-yield savings accounts can have an APY of 0.5%–1.15%. While it's still a relatively small yield, it's much higher than a traditional savings account. High-yield savings accounts also offer better compound interest. However, compared to traditional savings accounts, high-yield savings accounts can require larger deposits to open and have more limits on how much or how often you can withdraw money. Also, their APY usually isn't fixed, so if you sign on for an out-of-this-world rate, it may come back down to earth before long.

Treat Yourself—for Free: Go for a walk. Take one by yourself or connect with a friend. Listen to your surroundings or a podcast. However you do it, just get out. If it feels like a chore rather than a treat, think about this: walking regularly for at least 30 minutes a day is proven to boost your mood, improve your heart health, lower stress, and offer even more physical benefits. Now that's a treat.

"The greatness of a man is not in how much wealth he acquires, but in his integrity and his ability to affect those around him positively."

—BOB MARLEY

The Mason Jar Money Challenge

Also known as the 52-Week Savings Challenge, this plan has you put away a reasonably increasing amount of money each week of the year. In the end, you'll have more than $1,200 in savings.

How to do it: On New Year's Day, grab a mason jar—a big one. The first week of the year, put $1 in your mason jar. The second week, put $2 in. The third, add $3 . . . and so on each week of the year. While small dollar amounts may seem like no sweat, once you're adding twenties to your jar, you'll be giving your savings muscles a real workout. What's more, this challenge wraps up at the end of the year, so if you complete it successfully, you can really treat yourself (or others) come the holidays. Here's a tip: put a sticky note with 1–52 on your jar and tick off the weeks/dollars saved as you go.

Banks Versus Credit Unions

ere's the biggest difference between banks and credit unions: Banks are for-profit companies, and credit unions are nonprofit organizations run by their members. While they offer similar types of services, banks have the ultimate motivation of making a profit, whereas credit unions tend to focus more on their members' needs. As a result, banks can have more and higher fees, but they can also offer more products, services, and options. Since credit unions are run by and for their members, they may offer fewer products and have

more limited services, but they may also have fewer hurdles when opening an account. Here are some generalized pros and cons of each—though, always be sure to do your research and find out the particulars of any institution that claims to benefit you.

Banks	Credit Unions
+ More banking and investment options	– More limited banking and investment options
– Higher fees	+ Lower fees
– Lower interest rates	+ Higher interest rates
+ More branches, ATMs, and digital services	– More limited branches, ATMs, and digital services
– Less personalized service	+ More personalized service
+ Federally insured	+ Federally insured

Choosing or Changing a Bank

Before choosing or changing a bank, think carefully about the types of accounts you want to open right now, what your money habits are, and what your wealth goals are. There is no one-size-fits-all when it comes to banking. Your finances are as unique as you are. After analyzing where you are, what you do, and where you want to go, see how your results fit with the following banking items.

- **Offerings:** Do you need a basic account, or do you need more financial options? Ask about a bank's range of services for all your current and potential needs.
- **Fees:** Fees can lurk everywhere, from annual maintenance fees for checking accounts to overdraft fees to ATM fees. Think realistically about your habits and needs and how fees will affect you. Make sure your bank provides you with information about all its fees.
- **Minimums:** Banking minimums can show up in the form of a minimum deposit to open an account and a minimum balance needed in an account to avoid fees. Make sure to ask what minimums are required in any account

you need or might want in the future.

- **Location:** Banks can be national, regional, or local. They can have expansive networks of in-person locations and ATMs, or they can be more limited. Think about how much in-person banking you want to do, and how wide a network of branches and ATMs you want. Remember that there can be trade-offs for convenience: while you might save in ATM fees by using a bank with a large network, you might also pay a higher account fee.

- **Customer service:** Do you want in-person banking? Would a banking app on your phone help you stay on top of your budget? Do you mind spending time on hold when you have a banking issue? Find out how accessible your bank can be, and make sure you're comfortable with its customer service options.

- **Perks:** Let's face it; rewards, cash-back, and other incentives are nice to have. Compare perks across your banking options.

Interest and APR

An annual percentage rate, or APR, is the amount of interest charged on a loan. When you sign up for credit cards, they often tout a low APR. What they're saying is that they charge you a low rate on balances carried from month to month. It's important to know how your credit card company charges its APR—it can be on a monthly balance or a daily balance, and APR can be variable (changes) or fixed (doesn't change). All of these charges can really add up, so as much as possible, pay off the full balance at the end of each billing cycle. While it might feel counterintuitive, paying those bills on time can keep money in your pocket.

Credit Cards 101

With bank accounts, you draw down from the sum of money you deposited. Credit cards, on the other hand, let you borrow funds that you'll pay back when your bill is due. Sound like a dream come true? It can be. Credit cards are fantastic for building credit and allowing you to purchase big-ticket items, but they also come with some drawbacks.

THE CONS (AND PROS) OF CREDIT

There's good news and bad news when it comes to credit cards. Let's go with the bad news first. While credit cards make spending simple, they have the following—potentially major—pitfalls:

- **Fees everywhere:** Credit cards charge you interest on your credit card balances, but there are also annual fees, transaction fees, and late fees that can quickly add up. Make sure you're aware of all the fees that come with your card.
- **Debt adds up:** Unlike a debit card, where you're spending from your own money, with a credit card you're spending from a line of credit with a bank—they're essentially loaning you money that you must pay back. If you can't keep up with the minimum payments on your credit card, you'll have to pay that

money back *plus interest and finance charges*, digging further into your budget.

- **Dings to your credit score:** Credit history is a lifelong thing. Sure, it may not seem bad to miss a payment here or there, or to max out one card. But your credit decisions can follow you for life in the form of your credit score (see page 17).

Now for the good news:

+ **Spectacular scores:** Using credit wisely is reflected in your credit score, too. If you pay your bills on time and keep your balances in good standing, you'll have a higher credit score, which can help you with everything from getting a lower annual percentage rate (APR, see page 14) or a higher line of credit to renting an apartment, setting up utilities, and getting bank loans.

+ **Extra protections:** Credit card purchases can be backed by additional warranties and price protections. And you can be well protected from loss, theft, and fraud as long as they're reported quickly after they occur. Make sure to talk through all of your protections and policies with your credit card company.

Treat Yourself—for Free: Go to the library. You can satisfy that "need a new thing" craving with a stack of books, magazines, and more. Getting a library card is free and easy, if you don't already have one. Even better, local libraries are hotspots for community gatherings, author events, and learning opportunities. These places are practically bursting with free ways to treat yourself.

WHAT'S MY CREDIT SCORE?

A credit score is a three-digit number calculated by a credit bureau that reflects whether your credit history is very poor (300), perfect (850), or somewhere in between. While the exact cutoff varies depending on the credit bureau used, generally, a good score is 670, and a poor score is 600 or below.

Credit scores are calculated based on factors such as how much credit you use compared to your credit limit, whether you pay your bills on time, how many new credit card accounts you open, and your total credit mix (your credit cards, any loans, etc.).

Your credit score affects any financial area of your life where you might want to borrow money. A poor score means you might not be able to open credit cards, you might be denied loans, and you might even be denied housing rentals or get worse rates on car insurance, among other difficulties. Good and excellent credit scores allow you to apply for and make you more likely to get excellent credit cards that come with rewards and other advantages, like luxury travel upgrades and points for dining out. High credit ratings also mean better loan terms, easier and better mortgage applications and terms, and more.

Is your credit score in rough shape? Have no fear. Secured credit cards offer a way to get a credit card when your options are limited by making a deposit to establish your credit. Then, practice perfect credit behavior: pay your bills on time, don't carry a large balance, and spend within your means. All of this gets reported to credit bureaus, which in turn nudges your credit score back into favorable territory.

"Money never made
a man happy
yet, nor will it."

—BENJAMIN FRANKLIN

FIND THE RIGHT CARD FOR YOU

Don't just sign up for any credit card. Make sure the card in your wallet is the one that best aligns with your financial habits and wealth goals.

Prioritize cards with low or no APR if you . . .

- might occasionally carry a balance—don't pay more than you need to in interest;
- don't have a steady income—the chances you might miss a payment are higher;
- will carry the card for emergencies only.

Look for student or secured cards if you . . .

- are 18 years or older and want to open your first credit card;
- want to establish credit if you haven't done so before;
- have an unfortunate credit rating—these cards can help you improve your scores.

Seek out reward cards if you . . .

- pay your credit card bill in full every month and never carry a balance—in exchange for agreeing to a higher APR, these cards will give you perks for spending money;
- have good credit.

The Right Rewards

- **Cash-back:** These reward cards will put money back in your hands, usually at a rate of 1%, for the dollars you spend.
- **Cash-back categories:** A little more specific, these cash-back cards give you a percentage of your spending back in just one area, like groceries, gas, restaurants, or even Amazon.com orders.
- **Travel:** You'll be awarded points for flights, accommodations, and more depending on how much you spend. A credit card directly affiliated with an airline can also earn you mileage.
- **Even more perks:** Make sure to ask about what else your card can get you, including VIP access to special events.

Treat Yourself—for Free: Make a dream board. All you need are some scissors, glue or tape, old magazines and/or scrap paper, and some markers. Set aside some creative time and let your dreams and goals flow over you. Use your materials to create what living your dreams looks like to you. What words do you associate with achieving your wealth goals? What images inspire you? Make a collage of writings, drawings, and found images. Hang your dream board in a place where it can give you a boost when you need it most.

"It takes as much energy to wish as it does to plan."

—ELEANOR ROOSEVELT

BUILDING YOUR BUDGET

Setting Yourself Up for Success

W hat do you feel when you hear the word *budget*? For many, it can immediately spark feelings of deprivation, joylessness, and maybe even shame. Maybe it seems restrictive and suffocating. But take a deep breath and reset.

A budget doesn't need to feel stifling or limit you to cheap belongings or a bland lifestyle. The key is to create and stick to the right budget for you and your wealth goals. When you do that, a budget becomes a tool for financial independence, widens your options in the long term and in emergencies, frees you from endlessly hustling from paycheck to paycheck, gives you confidence that you have what you need, and improves your overall well-being. *Budget* sounds pretty great now, right?

Before You Break Out Your Spreadsheet . . .

Sure, money has a dollar value. But even more important is the value of what it can do for us. Money can mean security, peace of mind, and shelter; it can mean a wealth of experiences; it can afford you more options for living your life and providing care for the people you love.

Your goals for your money, and in a way, your life, are at the heart of any budget. Start by making

a list of what matters most to you, both right now and in the long term. Then use those items as guideposts for building your budget. For example, maybe your health matters to you, and you want to work toward feeling better physically—that could become a health and wellness part of your budget, where you plan for a gym membership and a trainer. Maybe security is what matters to you, so establishing an emergency fund becomes part of your budget. Maybe #1 on your bucket list is diving the Great Barrier Reef in Australia. How fun would it be to make that dream become a reality bit by bit every day through your budget?

Take a moment to listen to yourself and your heart, and make your list.

The No Spend Challenge

I n this challenge, you select an area of your financial life where you'll stop spending for a set amount of time. Yes, really—no spending at all!

How to do it: Determine what area of your typical spending you're going to shut down, and for how long. For example, you could spend no money on online purchases for a month, you could spend no money on new clothes for a season, or you could stop going out to restaurants for a month. The keys here are that you want to do your No Spend Challenge in an area where making changes will feel both good and doable, and do it for long enough to see your savings. Now, begin your challenge. Each day you succeed at spending no money in your given category, mark it off on the calendar. Once you've completed your challenge, quantify your savings, either by looking at your money habits from before and during the challenge to see what you've pocketed instead of spent or by doing some simple math. For example, if you decide to stop going to restaurants for a month, you could save $15 per meal. That really adds up!

Budget Basics

A budget has three main elements: what comes in, what goes out, and what you save. Grab a pencil or open your spreadsheet program, and let's get to work.

WHAT COMES IN: FIGURING OUT MONTHLY INCOME

Monthly income, very simply, is what money comes into your account every month. For most people, that's a paycheck. But you may have other monthly income streams, such as an inheritance, money from a side hustle, or other assets. Add your net income from your paycheck (see page 30) with these other revenue streams to figure out your monthly income.

ANATOMY OF A PAYCHECK

We love paychecks for that lump sum that shows up in our account every month. But give your paycheck the respect it deserves by learning the sum of its parts and what it means for your financial life. After all, you *earned* it.

1 **Pay period:** The pay period is displayed as a date range that aligns with the schedule your employer pays you on (e.g., if it's biweekly, you'll see a two-week date range displayed in the pay period setting).

2 **Gross income:** Your gross income is what you get paid before taxes are taken out. Gross income also doesn't reflect deductions.

3 **Net income:** This is the money that you get to deposit right now. Net income is the total income you have after taxes and deductions.

4 **Deductions:** These are the funds that are taken out of your gross income. They include the following:

- Federal and state income taxes: Taxes are taken out—or withheld—from your paycheck each pay period. (You might be thinking, *No fair!* But the good news is that you won't get a shocking tax bill come tax day.)
- Social Security: American employers and

workers contribute to the Social Security program, which gives retirement and disability benefits to employees.

- Medicare: These deductions contribute to the Medicare program, which provides medical benefits to people 65 and older and people with disabilities.
- Other deductions: Contributing to a 401(k)? Have health insurance through your employer? These are the other types of things you'll see deducted from your gross income. A nice thing, these deductions come out before taxes, so they reduce the overall amount you do get taxed on.

5 **YTD:** This section shows your totals for the year to date. It usually shows your YTD gross income, net income, and deductions.

COMPANY NAME				EARNINGS STATEMENT			
Employee Name							
Social Sec. No.		**❶** Pay Period		Pay Date		Employee ID	
123-45-6789		8/01/22-8/15/22		8/22/22		101	
Income	Rate	Hours	Current Total	Deductions		Current Total	YTD Total
❷ Gross Income			200.00	FICA - Medicare		2.90	31.90
				FICA - Social Security		12.40	125.40
				Federal Tax		8.63	93.51
				State Tax		0.74	8.21
❺ YTD Gross Income	YTD Deductions	YTD Net Income		Total	**❹** Deductions	**❸** Net Income	
2,800.00	479.02	2,320.98		200.00	24.67	175.33	

"Balancing your money is the key to having enough."

—ELIZABETH WARREN

WHAT GOES OUT: FIGURING OUT MONTHLY EXPENSES

Feeling pretty good after figuring out your monthly income? Prepare yourself: it's time to figure out your expenses. This is where all that money that just came in, goes out. As intimidating as it may seem, getting a solid accounting of your monthly expenses is the key to creating a manageable budget and achieving your financial goals.

Expenses fall into three broad categories of things you need, things you want, and things you're saving for. Here's a list of common expenses to factor into your budget:

- Rent/mortgage—whatever you pay for that roof over your head
- Utilities
  - Electric
  - Water
  - Internet
  - Gas
  - Cable
  - Other

- Cell phone bill (and any other phone bills you might have)
- Groceries

- Transportation (e.g., gas, subway/bus fare)
- Childcare (e.g., daycare, nanny, after-school programs)
- Pet care (e.g., food, medications, vet visits, pet sitting/dog walking)
- Self-care (regular maintenance of yourself—haircuts, medications)
- Insurance:
    - Car
    - Life
    - Pet
    - Homeowners'
    - Health (if not already deducted from your paycheck)

- Subscriptions (e.g., streaming services, phone apps, magazines, subscription boxes)
- Memberships (e.g., gyms, museums)
- Debt (e.g., credit cards, student loans)
- Entertainment (e.g., dining out, season tickets, movies, coffee, non-necessity purchases)
- Retirement
- Emergency fund

It's helpful to calculate your expenses in categories rather than in one lump sum. Doing so allows you to examine, analyze, and tweak elements of your spending when needed.

Feeling overwhelmed? No need: now it's time to find the budgeting strategy that will put the power of your finances firmly in your hands.

Treat Yourself—for Free: Learn something for free on YouTube. Sign language, yoga, knitting, chef-level knife skills, even budgeting tips—if you're curious about it, you can find a video online about it. Why pay for a class when you can find experts offering to expand your world for free from the comfort of your couch?

Bad Habit Savings Challenge

Bad habits cost you—in more ways than one! The Bad Habit Savings Challenge helps you turn those costs into savings, *and* you get to feel better about yourself in the process.

How it works: Like the No Spend Challenge, the Bad Habit Savings Challenge involves not spending money on something. But this time, it's a bad habit you want to stop. Want to quit smoking?  Cut back on caffeine? Take a break from drinking? All of these habits have physical and mental costs as well as financial ones. For this challenge, instead of spending the dollar amount you would on your habit, put that same amount into a jar, envelope, or savings account. Your growing savings will be just one more bit of motivation to kick your habit for good. *And* you can treat yourself at the end of the challenge. How much do you stand to save? If you're kicking a weekly bag-of-chips habit, you can pocket at least $200 after a year.

The Budget for You

As we noted earlier, there's no one-size-fits-all budgeting framework. The one that works for you fits with your income, your spending habits, and your financial life both right now and in the future—and most of all, the budget for you is the one that feels doable *to you*.

Here are a few standard budget frameworks that financial experts recommend:

50/30/20 RULE

Great for beginners, budgeters with a goal of paying down debt

Here's a simple breakdown: Put 50% of your after-tax income toward the things you need (e.g., rent, groceries, medications); put 30% toward the things you want (e.g., movie tickets, books to read, coffee from Starbucks); and put 20% into savings or toward paying down any debt you're carrying. It's as easy as 1-2-3 (or, um, 50, 30, 20).

PAY YOURSELF FIRST

Great for people who want to pay down debt as quickly as possible or have sizable financial goals

Flipping the 50/30/20 rule around, this budgeting framework emphasizes savings or your financial goals rather than your basic necessities. Here, you first designate the lump sum you'll need to set aside from your income to meet your given financial goal—whether that's paying down debt or saving for that Great Barrier Reef dive. Whatever is left over you can divide among your monthly needs and wants.

THE ENVELOPE SYSTEM

Great for people who want to rein in spending (especially spending online or on credit), budgeters with hefty savings goals

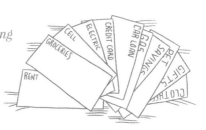

Need something a little more focused? For this cash-based budget system, you'll create categories of spending—however narrow you'd like them to be. For example, categories could be groceries this month, dining out, crafting supplies, gas, rent. Each category becomes an envelope that you fill with the cash allotted for that category that month. (You might want to analyze your spending for a month or two before using this budget framework so you have a sense of what's realistic to spend in each category.) Once you've spent everything in that envelope, you're completely done spending in that category until next month.

ZERO-BASED BUDGET

Great for people trying to get ahold of where their money goes each month, planners!

Inspired by a method of budgeting used by companies, a personal zero-based budget means that every month, you sit down with your after-tax income and subtract your planned expenditures in each expense category from that lump sum until you get to zero. That's your budget for the month. The key here is to revisit this exercise every month. If your zero-based budget is working, keep the same amounts in each expense category. If it's not or if you have something big coming up in a given month, switch it up and make different allotments. Unlike the cash-based envelope system, this budget approach allows you to use credit and debit cards and make online purchases—you just have to track every penny against your budget. This method allows for a rigid approach that can be flexible from month to month, and it encourages you to really analyze what works and doesn't work.

Treat Yourself—for Free: Rearrange your space. You may want a new couch or extra throw pillows or those curtains you saw on HGTV, but do you *need* them? Sometimes, just shaking up your room layout can make it feel like you've invested thousands in all-new décor.

Emergency Funds

Life has a way of surprising us—not always in a good way. And when it's bad, it's usually expensive. An emergency fund is an account where you can save money to use when the unexpected happens. It's not the same savings account you'll use for a down payment or to save for that bucket list trip. It should be separated from that entirely.

How much money you have in your emergency fund depends on many factors, like your essential expenses and whether you have dependents. You can find calculators online to help you tailor your emergency fund goal depending on your needs. Financial experts usually advise keeping at least three to six months' worth of income stored away for an emergency—but starting at any amount will help you in a pinch. Think about it: even if you can save $10 a week, you'll have $520 by the end of the year in your emergency fund. That money should be saved in a low-risk, interest-bearing account that you can access immediately if needed without incurring too heavy a fee for removing it—so a standard or high-yield savings account would be a good fit.

Make sure to allocate money for your emergency fund in your budget. You won't regret it.

How to Track Your Budget

Here's another moment on your wealth journey to stop and think deeply about yourself, your habits, and what works best for you. The best way to track your budget is a tracking system that feels manageable, fits with your life, and you will actually do! Ask yourself these questions:

Will I have more success meeting my budget if I track spending as it happens, daily, weekly, or monthly?

- Tracking spending as it happens can feel taxing and is easy to let slip in the moment, but if you can do it in real time, it gives you the tightest grip on your money. You'll be able to see in the moment how your purchases affect your goals.
- Tracking spending daily is also a commitment, but it allows you to reflect on patterns of spending in a day and see those near-real-time effects. It can also make you more motivated to make changes for the better the next day.
- Tracking weekly or monthly means you'll likely spend more time digging through account records and receipts, and you may

find that you've broken your budget without realizing it. But it spares you the to-do every day; forming a weekly or monthly habit is sometimes easier than creating a daily one.

Will I have more success tracking my spending if I do it in writing; in a spreadsheet, worksheet, or program; or using an auto-tracking app?

- Using old-fashioned pen and paper can be a helpful way to track expenses in the moment because you can always carry them with you and jot down information in real time. This method is also easily customizable.
- Entering expenses by hand into a spreadsheet, worksheet, or program is a great exercise for paying attention to your spending habits and seeing how they affect your goals. Spreadsheets have plenty of auto calculations and formatting options that can make your budget easy to use and appealing, as can apps. And worksheets can be helpful if you're a beginning budgeter, as they can guide you on how to best set up a

tracking sheet. The drawbacks? You may not have your tracker on you for in-the-moment updates.

- Some apps can link to your accounts and automatically sort your expenses into pre-defined spending categories, so you can see at a glance and with very little effort where your money is going. What you gain in efficiency might be lost in not being as closely attuned to your purchases—and there's always the possibility of missing a computer error.

Regardless of what system and cadence you use for analyzing your budget, make sure that at least monthly you take a moment to think about what's working, what isn't, and what you could do to improve the next month.

Treat Yourself—for Free: Sometimes budgeting can leave us feeling in a rut. Shake out of it by trying free trials. Don't have Hulu? Want to give a new spin class a spin? Investigate what trials are available to you, and get out there (or stay in and give streaming experiences a try). Just make sure to cancel before any fees kick in.

"Money is only a tool. It will take you wherever you wish, but it will not replace you as the driver."

—AYN RAND

Getting Everything in Order

As you comb through your financial life to set up your budget, take the opportunity to organize yourself. Maybe you have drawers of old paper statements you're just not sure whether to hold on to, or perhaps you found some old bank accounts that you thought you'd closed but apparently didn't. Now is the perfect time to declutter your money mess so you can be more organized and feel clearheaded when it comes to your financial well-being. Few things make you feel more in control than being able to immediately get your fingers on your financial information when you want it.

ORGANIZE AND . . .

To get your financial information organized, you'll need a folder on your computer and a few three-ring

binders, or folders and a drawer in your filing cabinet. Whatever system you use, make sure it's not overly complicated. You want to be able to quickly file what you need and quickly access it later.

What do you need to put in those folders? What can you get rid of? See *Purge Safely!*, page 48, for a quick guide, though you should always consult with your local tax resources and financial advisors for the best information for you and your financial situation.

. . . SIMPLIFY

Make your life easier! A few easy steps can ensure that your financial life is as streamlined as possible so you can focus on the things that matter most.

Automate and Autopay

Investigate your auto-options. Did you know that you can set bills to autopay? It saves you the time of sitting down to pay them, frees you from the mental load of thinking about the due dates, *and* it ensures you never have a late payment. Just make sure you have enough money in your account to cover everything you're autopaying.

Similarly, you can automate deposits into savings accounts and retirement plans—so you can save without lifting a finger.

Purge Safely!

Take care when trashing any financial documents! Your account numbers, Social Security numbers, and other details are for your and your financial expert's eyes only. Your best bet is to shred any personal documents with private information before purging them. You can buy a shredder anywhere you purchase office supplies. Alternatively, some banks, credit unions, and copy shops have shredders you can use, and some communities hold shredding events to help citizens ward against identity theft.

What You Can Purge

- **Credit card statements** can be purged after you reconcile the expenses and your payment clears.
- **Paycheck stubs** can be purged after a year.
- **Receipts** can be purged once you've reconciled them with your checking and credit card statements.
- **Bills** can be purged as soon as your payment clears.

What You Need to Keep

- Hold on to **tax records** for seven years; that includes returns but also receipts and anything supporting deductions.
- File any documents about a **home or property** you own for the duration of your ownership and at least seven years after; also hold on to any documents about what you spent buying or selling it.
- Keep records related to your **debt**—like student loans or mortgages—at least until you pay it off, but it can also be helpful to have records after the debt is paid should you need proof it's paid.

Combining Accounts

Have three credit cards? Four bank accounts? More savings accounts than you can count? Holding multiples of the same type of account gives you more to keep track of–which means you're not able to keep as close an eye on your money (not to mention the multiple rounds of fees). Combine accounts to simplify. Many financial experts recommend generally never having more than two of the same type of account to ensure you have maximum control.

Go Paperless!

Nearly every financial institution has the option to go paperless. Simply sign in to your account and look at your settings. Statements, bills, and notices can all be delivered electronically and accessed via your online account, which means you have access to all of your info with a click, *and* you have one less piece of paper lying around. Just make sure to store and organize your electronic statements and receipts in an easy and intuitive way on your own computer, and remember to back up your files.

Closing Old Accounts

In your decluttering project, you might have uncovered statements from an old retirement account that's just sitting there, or you might realize you have another credit card attached to your bank account. Close those accounts, pronto. There's no need—and actually it can be risky—to have open accounts you're not actively using or paying attention to. If you're not monitoring them or keeping close track of account information, it could fall into the wrong hands, or you could incur fees and charges you don't know about.

"It is not the creation of wealth that is wrong, but the love of money for its own sake."

—MARGARET THATCHER

GROWING WEALTH

Finding Your Path to Abundance

G rowing wealth begins with a healthy financial foundation. With smart day-to-day money management, control of your budget, and at least a solid start on an emergency fund, you may start thinking about other ways you can make your money work for you. You might level up by looking into investing.

Risks—and Rewards—of Investing

The adage "with great risk comes great reward" is a key principle in the world of investing. The rewards are clear: by investing your money, you stand to make more—sometimes lots more—with little effort on your part. The risks, on the other hand, can be numerous.

Often, in investing, the riskier the investment type, the higher the potential reward. Generally speaking, according to financial advisors, the longer before you need the money, the more risk you can tolerate. So when you're investing for retirement, if you're young, you can tolerate riskier investments early on and then gradually transfer your investments into lower-risk funds as you get older. That should net you the most return on your investment—but again, nothing is without risk when you're investing.

"Wealth is the ability to fully experience life."

—HENRY DAVID THOREAU

Let's take a look at a few common types of investments—also called asset classes—and their potential risks and rewards. Make sure to consult with a financial expert to find out what's best for you and to dig into the details of each investment type— that's super important when it comes to anything that puts your money at risk!

STOCKS

A stock, very simply, is a share in the ownership of a company. Companies sell stocks to raise funds so they can do things like expand into new markets or develop new products. If you buy stock in a company, you're a stockholder. Your stock can appreciate in value—meaning the price of the stock gets higher after you buy it—or depreciate in value (which is the opposite). The value of stocks rises and falls

depending on trading in the stock market, and it's also based on a company's performance and perceived value. You can make money when you buy a stock at a lower price and then sell it at a higher price. Stocks can also earn you dividends, which means a company is paying out some of the money it's made to its stockholders. Some stocks entitle stockholders to vote in company matters at shareholder meetings.

BONDS

You can think of a bond as money you're lending to an organization. In return for that loan, the organization promises to pay back your initial investment at an agreed-upon time, plus it pays you interest on your investment. That interest gets paid out regularly, usually twice a year. Bonds are often issued by governments, municipalities, and companies.

Bonds can be a more comfortable investment for people with lower risk tolerance, because you're promised your initial investment back when a bond matures, or comes due, no matter what.

MUTUAL FUNDS

When you invest in a mutual fund, your money goes into a big pool with other investors' contributions. This big pool of money is invested by a company's

"If you have trouble imagining a 20% loss in the stock market, you shouldn't be in stocks."

—JOHN BOGLE

fund manager, and they aim to achieve the goals summarized in the fund's prospectus, which is basically a description of the fund and its history and how it hopes to perform. Similar to how individuals make money on stocks, mutual funds make money by selling securities at a higher price than they paid for them and by collecting dividends from those securities. If you invest in a mutual fund, you can receive dividend payouts from the fund when it receives money, or you can sell your shares in the mutual fund and make money if the price of the fund has increased since you bought it.

RETIREMENT ACCOUNTS

An easy way to start investing is to open a retirement plan. These are often lower-risk, largely hands-off ways to grow your wealth and save for the day when you don't have to work anymore.

If you're a salaried employee, your company probably has a 401(k) fund that you can invest in. Usually, you can arrange for your 401(k) contribution to automatically be taken out of your paycheck every month, and that sum is often taken out before taxes and rolled into the account. Employers often even offer a match: if you invest a certain percentage of your paycheck, they will add a contribution to your retirement fund as well. Talk through match options with your human resources department and find out how much you need to save to get your employer's match.

Your employer might manage your 401(k) account or give you investing options, or you might be in the driver's seat. In any case, remember that you can usually tolerate more risk when you have more time before you want the money. So you can invest in higher-risk funds while you are far away from retirement. Manage your risk by diversifying and avoiding funds with big fluctuations. You can find retirement plan calculators online, and of course, professionals can help guide you in making wise retirement investments.

If your employer doesn't have a 401(k) or you want to open a retirement account on your own, look into an individual retirement account, or IRA. You can manage an IRA on your own, without an employer involved. You can hold both a 401(k) and an IRA at the same time.

Retirement funds frequently allow your money to grow without being taxed: your contributions can be made before tax, and you don't get taxed on the interest you earn. But you can incur taxes and other penalties if you take money out of a retirement account early. So as much as you can, leave that nest egg alone.

You Can Take It with You

Worried about what happens to your 401(k) if you leave your employer? Don't be! You can roll your money into another tax-deferred account rather than take it out.

How to Manage Risk

Unfortunately, risk is part of the deal when investing. But financial experts recommend a few tactics that can help minimize it.

- **Asset allocation** means dividing the funds you want to invest across a few different categories of assets. Doing this lessens the risk that you'll lose a lot if one asset class doesn't perform well. So, for example, you could put some money into stocks, some in real estate, and some in retirement accounts. If the real estate market tanked, you'd still have money in stocks and retirement accounts.

- **Diversification** means spreading your funds within an asset class. So instead of putting all your money into one stock, you spread it around among a few different types of stocks. The same rationale as in asset allocation applies here: if one stock plummets, you have other stocks that hopefully stay stable or grow.

Risks, ranked

High risk:
Futures, collectibles, stock options

Moderate risk:
Stocks, mutual funds, real estate

Low risk:
Bonds

Little to no risk:
Cash, CDs, savings accounts, insurance, treasury bills

Top 10 Money Mistakes, According to Financial Experts

1. Overspending

2. Not making a budget

3. Buying on credit

4. Only paying minimums

5. Not having an emergency fund or not having enough in it

6. Living paycheck to paycheck

7. Not knowing your credit score

8. Buying new instead of used

9. Forgetting about retirement

10. Paying down debts with low interest rates before those with high rates

Treat Yourself—for Free: Treat yourself while helping the world around you by volunteering. What do you get out of it? Research shows that volunteering can connect you with other people, reduce feelings of depression, and even positively affect your physical health and help you live longer. Volunteering can be as simple as reading to a young child, walking a

 dog, or stuffing envelopes. To find volunteer opportunities near you, search online for your location and what you're interested in, or look up local community organizations.

Money and Your Mindset

You might realize that certain feelings come up as you work through your budget and consider what level of risk you feel comfortable tolerating in your investments. Let's face it: Money is about more than math. It invokes powerful emotions—both positive and negative—and those feelings can be deeply tied to who we are and who we want to be, our memory, and our future. Whether money matters make you feel confident, ashamed, overwhelmed, successful, or any number of other emotions, those feelings can influence your actions. Having negative associations with money can result in negative financial outcomes.

You may have an unhealthy money mindset if any of the following are true:

- **Shame about debt.** Being in the red can deeply affect self-confidence, and that can turn into a reluctance to face the problem.
- **Fear about scarcity.** If you have ever felt like you or your loved ones have had to scrape together every last cent to pay the bills, you might have anxiety when it comes to making and spending money.
- **Guilt over not giving more away.** Especially if the people in your life aren't on the same financial footing as you, there could be guilt over not doing more, giving more, or helping more.
- **Confusion about saving and investing.** Money has its own terminology and systems and math, and that can be intimidating. Feeling overwhelmed can lead you to shut down in the face of your finances.

HOW TO HAVE A HEALTHIER
MONEY MINDSET

Do you see any of these unhealthy money mind-sets in yourself? If so, you've already taken your first step to a healthier approach to your finances. Next, working through these steps can help you change your mindset:

1. **Name it.** Search within yourself and name what you're feeling. Is it shame, guilt, fear, anxiety, or something else?
2. **Think about it.** Try to figure out what experiences or memories are prompting your feeling. Perhaps you felt less well off than your peers when you were growing up, so you feel anxious about money now. Maybe you regret an irresponsible spending spree and feel shame about that. Being aware of what fuels negative feelings about money helps you know what's motivating your actions—and that's the first step to getting control.
3. **Listen to the numbers.** Does your budget confirm or upend what your feelings are telling you? If you feel like you don't have enough, but the math checks out, that could be your anxiety. Whatever the numbers say, adjust your budget or behavior accordingly.

Money Mantras

Money matters can be overwhelming, and it's easy to feel discouraged as you work toward your financial goals. Pay attention to your mind. When you need a boost, try these abundance mantras. Repeat each one in between deep breaths. It can also help to stand in front of a mirror and look your reflection in the eye. Most of all, remember: you are worthy.

- I am open to wealth in whatever form it comes.
- I deserve prosperity. I attract it and respect it.
- I cultivate abundance in my every thought and deed.
- When one door closes, another one opens.
- My riches are vast and priceless, and I am grateful for them.
- Abundance is a mindset.
- I am worthy of everything I receive, work for, and hope for. I am worthy.

Upping Your Income

Investments are just one way to grow your wealth. You can also increase your income through your day job and through active and passive side jobs. Here are some ideas to think about.

KNOW YOUR WORTH
One of the first places to look for opportunities to increase your income is at your current job—and that starts with knowing your worth. First, get a sense of what other people who hold your position make. Compare your salary with information you can find online (the Bureau of Labor Statistics Occupational Outlook Handbook is a great place to start), from colleagues (if possible!), and from recruiters. How does it stack up? If you're getting paid less than your research suggests you should be, think about why that might be.

"Do the one thing you think you cannot do. Fail at it. Try again".

—OPRAH WINFREY

The Pantry Challenge/ No Dining Out Challenge

See how far you can stretch your grocery budget—and your culinary skills—by doing the Pantry Challenge. It's a great way to get all the value out of your food purchases and save some money while you do it.

How it works: Every now and again, skip your weekly grocery run and prepare meals only with what's in your pantry. Combine this with the No Dining Out Challenge (where you don't go out to restaurants or order takeout) for maximum savings.

WHEN TO ASK FOR A RAISE

If you're not making as much as your research suggests is fair, it might be time to talk about a raise. And timing can be everything. Certain scenarios can make it easier to broach the topic of getting a raise—and easier to actually get one:

- **You knocked it out of the park.** If you won a big piece of new business, got major kudos from an important client, or reconfigured a workflow to save time or money, you can highlight your achievements and see how your employer thinks that translates in terms of compensation.
- **Your performance reviews are stellar.** Getting above-average or excellent marks in your job performance? Great performance reviews show that your company values your performance—and a great way to show that value is in a raise, don't you think?
- **You're doing more for them.** Taking on another project on top of your workload, managing a new addition to your team, or getting a title bump can easily merit more pay.
- **It's been a minute since your last raise or salary adjustment.** Generally, most employers increase salaries by 3% per year to

adjust for inflation and other factors. Has your pay not moved in three years? It might be time for a talk.

- **You've got another offer.** This is leverage, friend. Use it!

Treat Yourself—for Free: Maybe you can't afford to jet off to the Maldives right now. But don't let that stop you from planning and researching your dream destination. Armchair travel is a budget-friendly way to explore the world without leaving your house. Pick your location and do a deep dive. Go beyond thinking about flight and lodging logistics, and look into local customs, research mom-and-pop shops to visit, learn the local language, and even find novels set in your dream locale. By the time you've filled up your vacation savings account, you'll be able to enjoy a trip like you've never had before thanks to all your planning and research ahead of time.

HOW TO NEGOTIATE A RAISE

If you've determined it's time to ask for a raise, make sure you're prepared when you meet with your higher-ups.

- **What's your goal?** By knowing your worth and what salaries in your position and industry look like, and by preparing a list of all you bring to the table, you can determine what you think is a fair raise to ask for. Start high in any discussion of your salary.
- **What's acceptable?** Think in ranges, not a single number. Though you should start high in your negotiations, having a range in mind will help you keep the discussion going if they don't agree to your top number out of the gate. Even a salary bump to the low end of your goal range is still a big win.
- **What could you compromise on?** Money isn't the only benefit to negotiate. Would you settle for a lower salary bump if that came with extra vacation days, a different schedule, stock options, or something else?

After thinking through these questions, prepare your pitch and practice the discussion with your loved ones before the real deal.

If your manager agrees that you should get a raise, suggest the highest end of your range. Try not to accept their counter right away, if they offer one. Instead, suggest a counter number closer to your original suggestion that's between yours and theirs.

SAVE YOUR RAISE

Go out to a fancy dinner to celebrate your salary bump! *Then* get to work saving your raise. (We heard that groan, but hear us out!) People tend not to change their savings plans even when they start making more money, according to financial advisors, and that can leave a gap between how you're used to living and the money you have to live on when it comes time to use your savings. Some financial experts recommend that you "save your age from your raise"—which means that you convert your age to a percentage, and save that much from your salary bump. Are you 25? Save 25% of your raise. Others suggest saving 33% of your raise, no matter what.

Happy Holiday Challenge

Does spending money on gifts at the end of the year sometimes leave you saying *bah humbug*? If so, try the Happy Holiday Challenge—saving ahead of time can ease that end-of-the-year crunch.

How it works: Decide how much you want to spend on gifts for family and friends during the holidays. (To help you gauge your shopping plans, according to National Retail Federation data,  Americans usually plan on spending about $1,000 on holiday gifts.) Take your gift goal and divide that total by how many weeks are left until the holidays to find out how much money you need to save each week. Then, put away your weekly savings target—ideally in an interest-bearing account, but mason jars and envelopes work, too.

If you celebrate Christmas and start your Happy Holiday Challenge at the new year, you'll need to put away $20 per week to reach a $1,000 goal. If you start with the same holiday and goal but begin on June 1, you'll need to save $30 per week.

Forget About the Grind;
Get a Successful Side Hustle

A side hustle is a way to make money outside of your main source of income. Are you thinking, *Wait, you want me to do a job in addition to my job-job?* Well, no. A side hustle isn't for everyone. But if you have a hobby that you love, an area that interests and excites you, a talent that you want to nurture, or a career path you want to consider switching to someday, a side hustle might be for you.

FINDING THE RIGHT SIDE HUSTLE FOR YOU

More than a job, a side hustle means getting paid for something you *choose* to do outside of your day job—so make your side hustle something you love. It also helps to be good at your side hustle—because that makes it easier to monetize. Your side hustle could be a product that you create based on your talent, services you offer based on your expertise, or something you enjoy doing. (See *Side Hustle Inspo*, page 80, to jump-start your brainstorm.)

Treat Yourself—for Free: Take a long, hot bath. Sounds simple, but make sure you really indulge: light candles, burn some sage, set the mood with some calming music, and create soothing scents with essential oils. You can turn your bathroom into a meditative spa. Don't skimp on postbath pampering, either. Lotion, face mask—the works! You deserve it.

Side Hustle Inspo

Not an amazing knitter or secret sculptor? Don't worry: there's a side hustle out there for you no matter what. Here are some ideas to get you thinking:

- Ad sales
- Babysitter
- Content creator
- Courier
- Dog walker
- Freelance designer
- Freelance social media maven
- Freelance writer
- Gig musician
- House cleaner
- Lawn mower/ landscaper
- Notary
- Property manager
- Ride-share driver
- Social media book reviewer
- Task handler (via services like TaskRabbit)
- Tutor
- Virtual assistant
- Wedding officiant

MAKING IT A SUCCESS

Take it from side hustlers who have been there, done that—there are a few keys to making your side hustle worth it.

- **Take baby steps.** No need to go all in. Getting your hustle up and running bit by bit will help you get a sense of what you need—energy, resources, time—both to balance it with your other responsibilities and to scale it up.
- **Keep those files.** Make sure you have detailed records of income from your side hustle and the expenses needed for it. All of that will be very important come tax time.

- **Set realistic goals.** You don't have to live off your side hustle (not right away, anyway!). Figure out why the time and effort you put into it benefit your life. Maybe your side hustle is what pays for your plane tickets for great vacations, or maybe walking dogs is a stress reliever that you just happen to get paid for—and that fills your emergency fund.
- **Put _you_ first.** Your side hustle is the icing on the cake. If at any point it's interfering negatively with your day job or your wellness, it's time to tone it down. The most successful side hustle is the one that you can maintain easily and that adds to your life.

"Without labor
nothing prospers."

—SOPHOCLES

Passive Income Possibilities

assive income streams can be a dream—they're a way to make money with little effort. Unlike a side hustle, there's little to no hustle involved in generating passive income outside of your setup efforts. What can earn you passive income? Here are some ideas:

Rent your home. You've probably been a guest at an Airbnb, Vrbo, or another rental at some point in your life. Turn your abode into a money-earning proposition by becoming a host yourself.

Advertise on your car. Earn money while you drive around town running errands. Some companies will pay you to put advertising on your car in the form of a magnetic or electronic sign.

License your creative work. Are you a writer, photographer, designer, or artist? Make a deal with a licensing agency and earn money from people using your work in their creations. You just get to sit there and earn money while your work spreads through the world!

Do affiliate sales. If you have a substantial audience online, consider affiliate sales. For most affiliate sales arrangements, all you have to do is agree to post a link or ad to another company's product on your social media, website, or blog. If someone clicks through the link you shared or uses a code unique to you, you'll get a portion of the sale.

ABOUT THE AUTHOR

L **eah N. Miles** is a writer and editor who loves a limited-time No Spend Challenge and devotes a healthy portion of her monthly budget to buying books. She lives in Atlanta with her son, husband, and cats.

Check out our other titles in
THE LITTLE BOOK OF *collection.*